On the Front Lines

The U.S. Army Rangers at War

by Michael and Gladys Green

Consultant:

Steve Maguire CPT, U.S. Army (Retired)
Vice President
U.S. Army Ranger Association

CAPSTONE HIGH-INTEREST BOOKS

an imprint of Capstone Press
Mankato, Minnesota

Capstone High-Interest Books are published by Capstone Press
151 Good Counsel Drive, P.O. Box 669, Mankato, Minnesota 56002
http://www.capstone-press.com

Green, Michael, 1952–
    The U.S. Army Rangers at war / by Michael and Gladys Green.
    p. cm.—(On the front lines)
    Includes bibliographical references (p. 31) and index.
    Summary: Chronicles the history, participation in armed conflicts,
weapons, and demanding training of the United States Army Rangers, a
small elite group of Army light infantrymen who perform short missions
behind enemy lines.
    ISBN 0-7368-2158-9
    1. United States. Army—Commando troops—History—Juvenile literature.
[1. United States. Army—Commando troops—History.] I. Title: The
United States Army Rangers at war. II. Green, Gladys, 1954- III. Title.
IV. Series.
UA34.R36G74 2004
356'.167'0973—dc21   2002155526

Editorial Credits
James Anderson, editor; Steve Christensen, series designer; Jason Knudson, book
    designer; Jo Miller, photo researcher; Karen Risch, product planning editor

Photo Credits
AP/Wide World Photos/David Weaver, 4
Corbis, 28; Baldwin H. Ward & Kathryn C. Ward, 10; Bettmann, 13; Reuters
    NewMedia Inc., 23
Defense Visual Information Center, 8, 14, 16, 24
Getty Images/DOD Photo, 26; Erik S. Lesser, 6; Scott Nelson, 20; U.S.
    Army/Mitch Frazier, cover

1 2 3 4 5 6 08 07 06 05 04 03

Table of Contents

CHAPTER 1

Learn about:

- **Parachuting**

- **75th Ranger Regiment**

- **Missions**

Rangers are trained as expert parachuters.

U.S. Army Rangers

On the coldest day of the winter, a commander tells his Rangers in training that it is time to learn how to jump from an airplane. The troops have been training for this day for weeks. They have done exercises. Their legs are strong from jumping out of trees in the woods.

On the airplane, the commander gives the final orders. Each trainee is to jump from the plane as quickly as he can. Once he hits the ground, the future Ranger is to bundle up his parachute. The trainees must then hike several miles to a camp in the woods. Their parachuting skills will be needed when they jump into their first combat zone.

Who are the Rangers?

The Rangers are a small group of about 2,000 U.S. Army soldiers. They form the 75th Ranger Regiment. They are an important part of the U.S. Army Special Operations Command (USASOC). The USASOC includes some of the most skilled soldiers in the U.S. armed forces.

The 75th Regiment is made up of three battalions. The 1st Battalion is based at Hunter Army Airfield in Georgia. The 2nd Battalion is based at Fort Lewis, Washington. The 3rd Battalion's base is located at Fort Benning, Georgia.

Each Ranger battalion has up to 660 men. Battalions are divided into three groups called rifle companies. Congress does not allow women to serve in the Rangers.

Rangers are some of the most skilled soldiers.

Rangers carry few supplies on their missions.

Ranger Missions

Ranger missions usually last only a few days. Rangers only carry five days' worth of supplies with them on their missions. Once a mission is finished, the Rangers return to their base. They begin training for their next mission.

A common Ranger mission is to capture or destroy enemy airports or seaports. Rangers also rescue people or equipment lost behind enemy lines.

Rangers are known for parachuting to their targets during short raids. U.S. Army Rangers have been expert parachute jumpers since the Korean War (1950–1953). Parachuting to a target is a good way to take an enemy by surprise.

Rangers often depend on other military forces. These other forces are called upon to attack larger enemy units once the Rangers have completed their mission.

Close Air Support (CAS) is provided by U.S. forces. CAS troops often help transport Rangers to and from battle areas. Rangers may also call on Army helicopter gunships or naval gunfire support for assistance.

CHAPTER 2

Learn about:

- Rogers' Rangers

- Vietnam

- Operation Just Cause

Rogers' Rangers was the first Ranger unit.

Ranger History

The name Army Rangers comes from "Rogers' Rangers." This British force fought during the French and Indian War (1754–1763).

Rogers' Rangers

Rogers' Rangers was named after Major Robert Rogers. His unit performed many raids during the French and Indian War. Major Rogers trained his men to live and fight in the woods for long periods of time.

Rogers' Rangers split up after the war. New Ranger units were formed during the Revolutionary War (1775–1783). Rangers also served in the Mexican War (1846–1848) and the Civil War (1861–1865).

World War II

America entered World War II (1939–1945) in December 1941. The U.S. Army again needed well-trained troops to send into enemy territory.

In June 1942, the 1st Ranger Battalion was formed. More Ranger units were formed in 1943.

The most famous Ranger battalion in World War II was Merrill's Marauders. The group was named after General Frank M. Merrill. These men walked more than 1,000 miles (1,600 kilometers) through a jungle to fight a battle.

Korean War

During the Korean War, the Army formed new Ranger units. These expert parachuters were called Airborne Ranger Companies.

Nearly 700 men signed up to be part of the new Airborne Rangers. The Army formed six Airborne Ranger groups. These Rangers jumped from airplanes onto the cold mountains of Korea.

Rangers fought many battles in the Korean War.

Vietnam War

During the Vietnam War (1954–1975), the Army turned some of its soldiers into Ranger Companies. These units monitored enemy radio signals and set up ambushes.

Rangers were successful in Vietnam. After the war, military leaders made the Rangers a permanent part of the U.S. Army.

Grenada

The next Ranger mission came in 1983. Rangers were ordered to invade the small Caribbean island of Grenada. The government in Grenada had taken U.S. citizens hostage.

Rangers arrived in Grenada in 1983.

The mission was named Operation Urgent Fury. Rangers dropped by parachute to capture an airport. They rescued American college students who were being held there.

Panama

In December 1989, Rangers took part in Operation Just Cause. The U.S. military invaded the Central American country of Panama.

The United States wanted to force a corrupt dictator from power. Army Rangers helped early in this operation by taking over an airport in Panama.

CHAPTER 3

Learn about:

- ■ **Rangers in Kuwait**

- ■ **Somalia**

- ■ **Fight against terrorism**

Rangers participated in Operation Desert Storm

Recent Conflicts

The Middle Eastern country of Iraq invaded the country of Kuwait on August 2, 1990. The U.S. government decided to help free Kuwait from Iraqi control.

Operation Desert Storm

U.S. ground forces arrived within a week of the Iraqi invasion. On January 17, 1991, U.S. planes attacked Iraqi forces. This attack was part of Operation Desert Storm.

In February 1991, a small force of Rangers secretly crossed into Kuwait and Iraq. They gathered Iraqi military secrets. Soon after the Ranger missions were completed, U.S. ground troops attacked the Iraqi army.

Four days later, the Iraqi army went back to Iraq. Kuwait was free again. Information provided by the Army Rangers helped defeat the Iraqi army.

Operation Task Force Ranger

On October 3, 1993, Rangers launched a daytime helicopter raid in Somalia. Two groups in this country had been at war since 1977. Somalia's last leader left in 1991. Armed gangs then took over the country. Somalia had no government, army, or police force.

Rangers attacked an armed gang headquarters. As the Rangers left the enemy's buildings, two U.S. helicopters were shot down. Rangers tried to save the crew of the fallen helicopters. The Rangers were quickly surrounded by thousands of attacking gang members.

Some Rangers and other U.S. forces died. But most of the helicopter crew members were rescued.

Operation Enduring Freedom

Terrorists attacked New York City and Washington, D.C., on September 11, 2001. Thousands of Americans and foreign visitors died in the attacks.

The terrorists' home base was in Afghanistan, a country in central Asia. A group called the Taliban ruled the country. The Taliban would not turn over the terrorists to the United States.

Important Dates

1754—French and Indian War begins. Major Robert Rogers forms Rogers' Rangers.

1942—1st Ranger Battalion formed.

1950—Korean War begins. Airborne Ranger Companies formed.

1969—Ranger Companies are formed during the Vietnam War.

1983—Operation Urgent Fury begins.

1989—Operation Just Cause takes place.

1991—U.S. military participates in Operation Desert Storm.

1993—Operation Task Force Ranger takes place.

2001—Terrorists attack New York and Washington, D.C., on September 11. Rangers are sent to Afghanistan.

2002—Operation Anaconda begins in Afghanistan.

2003—U.S. and Allied forces take part in Operation Iraqi Freedom.

Rangers searched for and fought terrorists in Afghanistan.

To stop more terrorist attacks, the U.S. military invaded Afghanistan. U.S. planes began to bomb the country on October 7, 2001.

On October 19, more than 100 Rangers parachuted into Afghanistan at night. Their targets were a Taliban headquarters and a small airport.

During the raids, Rangers destroyed Taliban weapon storage sites. They also overtook 43 Taliban members. Most Taliban soldiers ran away into the dark.

Rangers returned to Afghanistan a few months later. This time, their mission was to find terrorists who were hiding. The Rangers searched caves in the mountains. They captured many terrorists and weapons.

Operation Anaconda

In March 2002, the U.S. military launched Operation Anaconda. The purpose was to destroy terrorist forces hiding in the mountains of Afghanistan.

On May 9, enemy terrorist troops attacked just as the first Rangers in U.S. helicopters arrived. Rangers called in air support. After 10 days of fighting, the operation was called a success.

Operation Iraqi Freedom

U.S. and Allied forces began Operation Iraqi Freedom in March 2003. Ranger missions included securing Iraqi air bases and oil fields.

Javelin Antitank Missile

Function:	Antitank weapon
First Deployed:	1996
Firing Range:	1.2 miles (1.9 kilometers)
Weight:	23 pounds (10.4 kilograms)
Length:	47.2 inches (119.9 centimeters)

In the late 1980s, work began on a new antitank missile. It was called the Javelin. Testing of the new missile began in 1993. Rangers started using the weapon in 1996.

The Javelin is made up of the Command Launch Unit (CLU) and the missile. The CLU has a sighting system. This system allows the gunner to see targets day or night.

The gunner and the loader are the two men on a Javelin team. The gunner carries the CLU. The loader carries extra missile containers.

The Javelin is a fire-and-forget weapon. The gunner sees the target and fires. The missile will guide itself to the target. The missile finds heat generated from the enemy tank's engine.

CHAPTER 4

Learn about:

■ Helicopters

■ M4 rifle

■ Training

Rangers can be involved in missions in any part of the world.

There is always a Ranger batallion on alert. Rangers can get to anywhere in the world in just 18 hours.

Ranger Weapons

Rangers carry a M4 rifle. This weapon fires three shots each time the trigger is pulled. The M4 has a single-shot 40mm grenade launcher, a laser pointing device, a silencer, and a system for seeing in the dark.

Rangers also use the M249 Squad Automatic Weapon (SAW) machine gun. It was specially designed for the Rangers. The M249 is made to be fired from a standing position.

M224 60mm Lightweight Mortar

- **Function:** Short Range Fire Support
- **Date Deployed:** 1990s
- **Firing Range:** 3,817 yards (3,490 meters)
- **Weight:** 46.5 pounds (21.1 kilograms)

The Army used its first 60mm mortar in 1940. It was called the M2. A crew of two men operated the M2. It had a range of 1,985 yards (1,815 meters).

In the 1990s, the Army began to use the M224. Like the M2, it is operated by two men. The M224 can hit targets within 3,817 yards (3,490 meters).

The M224 mortar fires three types of ammunition. They include high explosive, smoke, and illumination.

High explosive ammunition kills people, and smoke hides people. Illumination is used at night. It lights up an area so that Rangers can see their targets.

Ranger Aerial Transportation

Rangers parachute to targets from Air Force transport planes. Army helicopters also bring Rangers to their target areas.

Rangers use motorcycles on some missions.

Helicopters deliver Rangers without landing. Rangers slide to the ground on long ropes. They wear thick gloves to protect their hands.

Motorcycles

On the ground, Rangers sometimes use motorcycles to get around. The motorcycles are Kawasaki KLR250s. Rangers use them for scouting and for delivering messages.

Ranger Training

All Rangers are volunteers. Anyone who wants to be a Ranger must go through long training and pass difficult physical tests.

If a hopeful Ranger passes advanced training, he is sent to a three-week parachute school. After learning to parachute, the soldier goes to three more weeks of training. If he passes, he can join the 75th Ranger Regiment.

The final step is a tough 62-day Ranger school. Upon completion, the Ranger is awarded a Ranger patch for his left shoulder.

Rangers are always prepared for conflicts. When trouble breaks out in some part of the world, the Rangers might be the first U.S. forces to arrive.

Words to Know

battalion (bat-TAL-yun)—a group of soldiers

headquarters (HED-kwor-turz)—the place where an organization is run

mission (MISH-uhn)—a military task

mortar (MOR-tur)—a short cannon that shoots small explosives in a high arc

parachute (PA-ruh-shoot)—a large piece of strong, lightweight fabric; parachutes allow soldiers to jump from airplanes and land safely on the ground.

silencer (SYE-luhn-sur)—an attachment for a gun that reduces noise when the gun is fired

transport (TRANSS-port)—to move people or supplies

To Learn More

Bryant, Russ. *To Be a U.S. Army Ranger.* To Be A. St. Paul, Minn.: MBI Publishing, 2003.

Burgan, Michael. *U.S. Army Special Operations Forces: Airborne Rangers.* Warfare and Weapons. Mankato, Minn.: Capstone Press, 2000.

Poolos, J. *Army Rangers: Surveillance and Reconnaissance for the U.S. Army.* Inside Special Operations. New York: Rosen, 2003.

Useful Addresses

U.S. Army Military History Institute
22 Ashburn Drive, Carlisle Barracks
Carlisle, PA 17013-5008

U.S. Army Public Affairs
Office of the Chief of Public Affairs
1500 Army Pentagon
Washington, DC 20310-1500

Internet Sites

Do you want to find out more about U.S. Army Rangers?
Let FactHound, our fact-finding hound dog, do the research for you.

Here's how:

1) Visit *http://www.facthound.com*
2) Type in the **Book ID** number: **0736821589**
3) Click on **FETCH IT**.

FactHound will fetch Internet sites picked by our editors just for you!

Index